Twelve Poems of Emily Dickinson

set to music by Aaron Copland

voice and piano

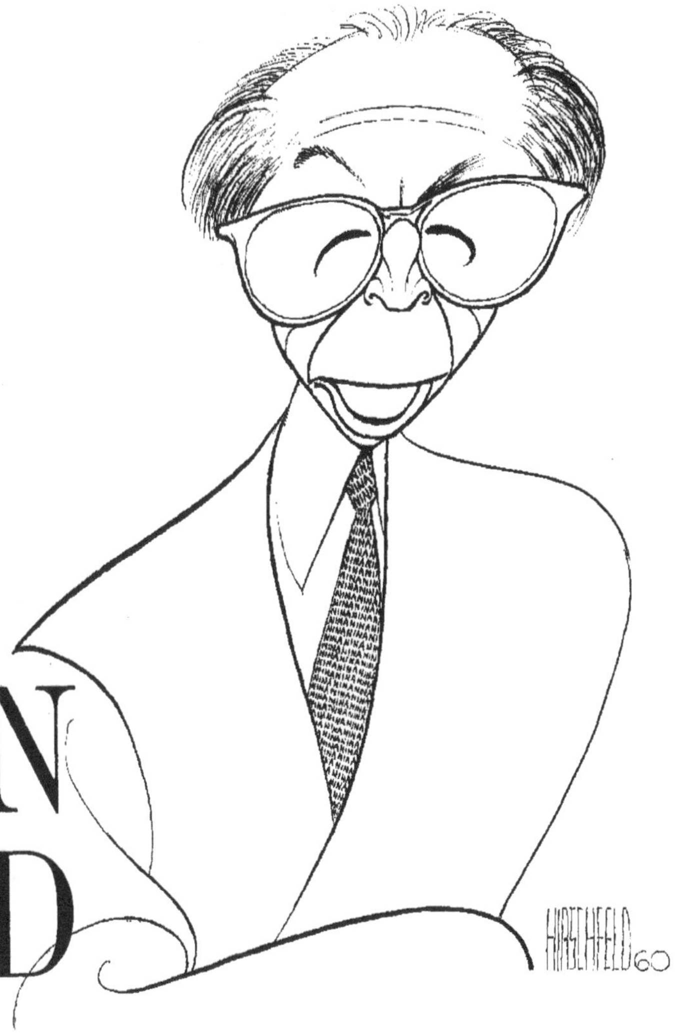

AARON
COPLAND

HIRSCHFELD 60

The composer has supplied the following information about **Twelve Poems of Emily Dickinson**: "These twelve songs were composed at Sneden's Landing, New York, at various times during the period from March 1949 to March 1950. They are the first works the composer has written for solo voice and piano since 1928.

"The poems centre about no single theme, but they treat of subject matter particularly close to Miss Dickinson: nature, death, life, eternity. Only two of the songs are related thematically, the seventh and twelfth. Nevertheless, the composer hopes that, in seeking a musical counterpart for the unique personality of the poet, he has given the songs, taken together, the aspect of a song cycle. The twelve songs are dedicated to twelve composer friends."

1. **Nature, the gentlest mother**
2. **There came a wind like a bugle**
3. **Why do they shut me out of Heaven?**
4. **The world feels dusty**
5. **Heart, we will forget him**
6. **Dear March, come in!**
7. **Sleep is supposed to be**
8. **When they come back**
9. **I felt a funeral in my brain**
10. **I've heard an organ talk sometimes**
11. **Going to Heaven!**
12. **The Chariot**

To David Diamond

1. Nature, the gentlest mother

Music by
AARON COPLAND

Printed in U.S.A.

moving forward - - - (♩= 69)

of no child .... The feeb - lest... or the way-ward-est

poetically

p

hold back - - - *mf*

Her ad-mon - i - tion mild .... In for - est and the hill .... By

mf

moving forward

trav-ell - er is heard Re - strain - ing ramp - ant

mp

squir - rel .... or too im - pet - u - ous

p

Hold back (♩= 63) - - - - - moving forward
(pastoral-like)
bird.
mf
mp
Faster (♩= 92)
mp
How fair her con-ver-sa-tion ....
A summer af-ter-
p
mp
p
more brightly
mf
-noon. ....
Her house-hold, her as - sem-bly
mp
p
mf
And when the sun goes down ....
Her

voice a - mong the aisles In - cites the tim - id prayer Of
the mi - nu-test crick-et The most un - wor - thy
mf
mf
sf
sf
f
molto rit.
flower.
(long)
ff
sff
tr
tr
ppp
sf
sf
As at first (♩= 60)
p
moving forward (♩= 69)
When all the chil-dren sleep, She turns as long a - way, As will suf -
p
pp
p

(Duration 3 mins. 50 secs.)

To Elliott Carter

2. There came a wind like a bugle

Music by
AARON COPLAND

Printed in U.S.A.

somewhat slower
rit. - - -
(short)
om - i - nous did pass. We
cresc. - - - - - - - - - - - - - - - - -
marc.
with emphasis
barred the win - dow and the doors As from an emerald ghost
(faster - - - - .)
l.h.
mp freely
The doom's e - lec - tric moc - ca - sin.... that ve - ry in - stant

a tempo (♩= 112)
passed.
mp
On a
ff
f marc.
dim.
mp
Ped.
Ped. sim.
strange mob of pant - ing trees and fen - ces fled a - way.
(♩= 104)
mf
And riv - ers where the
mp
(blurred)
8ba
Ped.
hous - es ran the liv - ing looked that day,
ff
8va
8va
ff (clangorous)
Ped.
Ped.

f
The bell..... with - in........ the stee - ple wild... The
8va
f
Ped. simile
As at first
fly - ing ti - dings whirled
ff sff sf
rit. - - - Broadly f with emphasis
How much can come And
Ped.
ff
much can go........ And yet a - bide the world.
ff
sf sf
8ba
(Duration 1 min.30 secs.)

To Ingolf Dahl

3. Why do they shut me out of Heaven?

Music by
AARON COPLAND

(Duration 1 min. 50 secs.)

To Alexei Haieff

4. The world feels dusty

Music by
AARON COPLAND

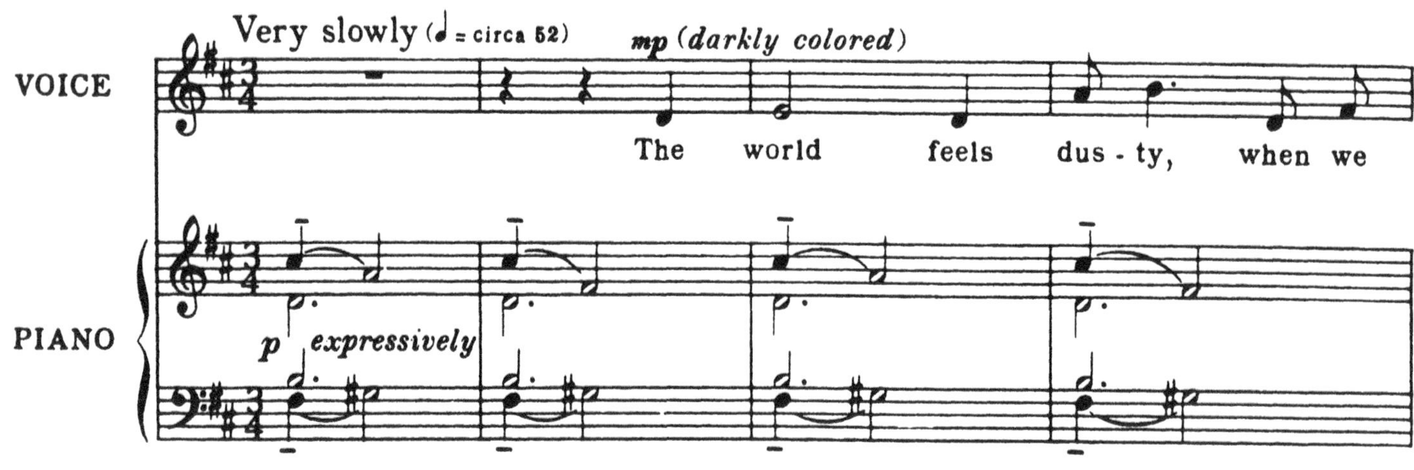

Printed in U.S.A.

(Duration 1 min. 45 secs.)

To Marcelle de Manziarly

5. Heart, we will forget him

Music by
AARON COPLAND

* Grace note on the beat

Printed in U.S.A.

(Duration 2 mins. 10 secs.)

To Juan Orrego Salas

6. Dear March, come in!

Music by
AARON COPLAND

How out of breath .... you are.
cresc.
r.h.
Dear March, how are you? ....
f
And .... the rest? ....
ff
meno f
sub. mp
Did you leave Na - ture well? .... Oh, March come right up -
mp
poco a poco cresc.

f
ff
- stairs with me I have so much to tell.
(cresc.)
ff marc.
poco rit.
(♩. = 112)
dim. molto
mp
p
I got your let-ter and the bird's
mp
The ma-ples ne-ver knew that you were com-ing,

I declare How red their fac-es grew,
poco sf
p
But March for-give me.
mf
mp
And all those hills you left for me to hue,
There
f
poco sf
mp
freely - - slowing up
was no pur-ple suit-a-ble,
mf
You took it all with
rit.

Tempo I (♩. = 116-120)
ff
you.
ff marc.
Ped.
p
Who knocks?
mp
that A-pril?
sub. ff
Lock the door,
mf
I will not be pur-sued
He stayed away a
Ped. sim.
f
year,
to call when I am oc-cu-pied
relax the tempo
dim. molto

(Duration 2 mins. 15 secs.)

To Irving Fine

7. Sleep is supposed to be

Music by
AARON COPLAND

Printed in U.S.A.

Sleep is the sta-tion grand Down which on
ei-ther hand The hosts of wit-ness stand Morn
is supposed to be, By peo-ple of de-gree
The break-ing of the day, Morn-ing
with emphasis
poco
marc.

* long pause before starting No. 8
(Duration 2 mins. 45 Secs.)

8. When they come back

Music by
AARON COPLAND

Printed in U.S.A.

p
When they be - gin .... if rob - ins
sub. p
* mark the l.h.
mf
do I al - ways had a fear I did not tell it
mf
f
was their last Ex - per - i - ment last year.
ff
f
When it is May,

if May re-turn.
sf
mf
Has no-bo-dy a pang that on a face so beau-ti-
mp
-ful we might not look a-gain.
p
poco marc. f
f
more deliberate
rit. molto
p calmly (𝅗𝅥 = 84)
If I am
f
f
ff
mp
f

(Duration 1 min. 40 secs.)

9. I felt a funeral in my brain

Music by
AARON COPLAND

Printed in U.S.A.

ritardando
ff
Slower (♩ = 63)
...... that sense .... was break - ing through ....(exaggerate the
ff
ff (thud-like)
mf (♩ = 60)
first beat of each measure) And when they all were seat - ed A ser-vice like a
mf, ma marc.
8
(secco)
drum Kept beat - ing, beat - ing, beat - ing till I thought my
più f
mind was go - ing numb. And then I heard them
sostenuto
più f
lift a box, And creak a - cross my soul With those same

mf

boots of lead a - gain, Then space be-gan to toll ....

(bell-like)

f–mf (poco marc.)

(mp) (mp) (sim.)

f

...... As all the hea-vens were a bell .... And Be-ing but an

f

p

ear. .... And I and si - lence

ff fff–p sostenuto

(p)

(the l.h. thud-like) (mf–sempre)

mf

some strange race Wrecked ....

mp p

soi - i - tar - y here. .... rit. - - - -

p pp morendo - - -

(Duration 2 mins. 10 secs.)

To Alberto Ginastera

10. I've heard an organ talk sometimes

Music by
AARON COPLAND

(Duration 1 min. 50 secs.)

To Lukas Foss

11. Going to Heaven!

Music by
AARON COPLAND

Printed in U.S.A.

an-swer-ing you
Going to
non legato
sub. f marc.
Heaven! Going to Hea-ven!
How dim it
rit.
sub. pp
a tempo
sounds
And yet it will be
p
delicately
done
As sure as flocks go home at night Un - to the shepherd's arm!
Ped. sim.

Slower (freely)
mf
Per-haps you're going too!
a tempo
...... Who knows? ....
sub. f
impetuous
f-mp
mf
If
you should get there first ..... Save just a lit-tle place for me, Close ....
sim.
ff sf
f
.... to the two .... I .... lost ....
mf
f sf
mp
mf sf
p

mp
The smallest "robe" will fit me.... and
just a bit of "crown" for you know we do not mind our dress when we ....
...... are go-ing home. ....
f freely
Going to
mp
Ped. *
senza Ped.
p
sub. ff non legato
sf

slowing up
Broadly – recitative style
sf
Hea-ven, Go-ing to Hea - ven! .... I'm glad I don't be - lieve it.... For
mp a tempo
it would stop my breath And I'd like to look a lit - tle more at
p
such .... a cu - ri - ous earth. ....
Slower, freely (♩. = 80)
mp
I am glad .... they did be - lieve it........
mp
p

(Duration 2 mins. 40 secs.)

12. The Chariot

Music by
AARON COPLAND

Printed in U.S.A.

More slowly (♩= 66)
mf
held but just our - selves .... and Im-mor - tal - i - ty................ We
p
mf
slow - ly drove .... He knew no haste and I had put a - way...
.... My la - bour....... and my lei-sure too For his ci - vil - i - ty........
poco f
mp
As at first (♩= 76)
p
....
mp
We passed the school where children

trifle faster (♩ = 88)
mf
played, Their les-sons scarcely done We passed the fields of
mf
f
ff
gaz - ing grain .... We passed .... the
cresc.
f
ff
Tempo I (♩ = 76)
poco sf
p
mp calm
set - ting sun, ... We paused be-
sostenuto, calm
poco sf
mp
p
sust. Ped.
mf
- fore a house that seemed a swell - ing of the ground ..... The
poco sf
mp
sust. Ped.

Please include full details of title, author, composer and publisher of this work on THE PERFORMING RIGHT SOCIETY'S returns whenever it is publicly performed.